Praise for **All tl**

MW00791849

In *All the Stars Aflame*, Malik Abduh journeys to various places in our history — shapeshifting, listening, bearing witness, and returning to the present to offer us impressions, portraits, the local evidence of rage and love. This debut collection is more than a decade in the making from a poet who composes with impressive scholarly attention, while remaining delighted in language and scene-making. Abduh's craft is spiritually attuned to a feverish love of justice. He points us to the patterns of the past which make a kind of music, so that all the fragments of these stories make a song—and that song burns with American history. I'm thrilled to finally see these poems in the world.

— Patrick Rosal

ALL THE
★STARS★
AFLAME

ALL THE ★STARS★ AFLAME

poems

M. Abduh

GETVAM
FRESH BOOKS

All the Stars Aflame

Get Fresh Books Publishing, A Non-Profit Corp.
gfbpublishing.org

ISBN: 978-0-578-31372-6

Library of Congress Control Number: 2021951114

Cover design: Mark Rosal
Cover image: The Philadelphia Citizen

for Green Bean & Rube

Contents

I

II

I

"Try to imagine how you would feel if you woke up one morning to find the sun shining and all the stars aflame."

— James Baldwin, *The Fire Next Time*

Atlanta, 1906

I

The New South congregated beneath an iron spire
pointing Godward, beneath John the Baptist,
his arms to the elbows in blue stained glass,
while the men along Decatur hunched over jugs
of corn whiskey & talked of virtue, talked & belched
the words of Tom Watson, who exhorted the crowds
to break the grip of the black fist strangling the throat
of the South. Someone, he said, had to speak:

The chopping block, men, the chopping block
for the head of the great Black Beast! Can't you hear
him scratching at your doors? Look at the monster's bloody chin,
your women & young ones like gristle between his jaws!
Cut off his Black Hand, clawing at your doors, reaching
for the purity of your women! You are the saviors of the South!
Like Jacob you must wrestle the Black Devil, wrestle
the Black Devil till your land is pure!

He told the story of some daughter of the South
who crossed the orchids, passing her basket
hand to hand, pecans piled almost to the handle.
Who dragged her into the burning bush?
The Black Hand drug her there!
The hand that tore her dress & blouse,
felt her moistness. The hand reaching
for the thigh of every daughter of the South.
Bring the dogs!
$800 for the head & hand of the Black Beast!
The barks of the hounds answered

3

from every woodland road, every backyard
& barnyard, until he (& any *he* would do) was
thrown down at her weathered porch,
condemned by the pointing of a finger.

Kill the Nigger! Keep your daughters pure!

The words of Watson drove the mob
across the land like locusts, burned like acid
in the sockets of their skulls.

II

They came with the taste of salt on their lips
from every porch in Georgia, ten thousand pilgrims
to that shrine, God-frenzied, spilling into Sydney's
barbershop to unload a revolver into his chest,
to leave him pulling at his vest like a man in fire.

The Sugar Creek Bridge shook beneath them
as they searched the black waters with oil lamps
for the beast they say devoured Mary Chafin.

In a train yard, a Black boy hid in a pitch-dark
cattle car under hay & cow shit & soaked his trousers
while the hounds panted beneath the rail wheels.

Down on Forsyth, a man drummed
to the chant of the mob:
Clean out the niggers!
For Mary, for Mary,
golden peach of the South!
They set their fires & prayed,

Good Lord, let them spread—
let them spread till Judgment Day.

Fire & brimstone & hell for 'em all.
Burn all them niggers to hell!

Red Summer, 1919

Dear Raymond,

It pains me to write you from so far, after so long.
But God is good, & it's like heaven up in Harlem
for a boy who can tickle the ivories.
Your last letter reached me just a week ago,
& I ain't at all surprised them sheriffs come
to Hoop Spur looking for bootleggers.
White folks know better than us that bootleggers
earn more than sharecroppers. Been the same every
city we play: Chicago, New Orleans, Tulsa.
They burnin' every farmhouse & outhouse from
Charleston to Knoxville. Our drummer Avery
say they hangin' colored folk down in Longview
like laundry. But I'm thankful that you & Mama
& Fat Baby are safe from all harm & danger.
Soon as the good Lord allow, I'll be home in Elaine.
Until then, I pray He keeps you & watches over you.

Your loving brother,

Samuel

Chicago, 1919

I

When the Windy City spread
the noon oppression, we bobbed
& splashed in Lake Michigan.

Along 25th Street, we dove & watched to
see who could hold their breath the longest.
Little Eugene always snuck a gulp of air & said,
I got the strongest lungs in Chicago.
We laughed & dunked him under to make him prove it.

He floated dead man across the lake to the spot
where the sweet water gets muddy,
where the white boys yell us niggers
are dirtier than catfish,

where one of them threw a stone & cracked
Eugene's skull like a dry plum pit, where he
floated dead man in blood-clouded sweet
water, & tried to sneak a hundred gulps of air
into the strongest lungs in Chicago.

Our fathers & mothers & cousins went
to the 29th Street beach to give them white folks
back their rocks. But James Crawford brought
a gun to a stone fight, & only then did the police
remove the thumbs from their belts. & that night
in Englewood, beside the glow of their
crosses, them whites vowed that the Black
Belt, too, would burn.

II

We walked the streets barefoot,
sat on the curb & stared into the black
mouth of his old house, & remembered
how Little Eugene tried to hold his breath.

Tulsa, 1921

I

The world outside Magic City was a knot—
your fingers cramped just trying to untie it.
But on Black Wall Street there was smothered
steak with rice & peas, & Little Rose's Beauty Salon,
where women winced under the hot comb sizzling
the back of their necks, the smell of lye rising from its teeth.

After oil flooded the Glenn family farm,
men like Bill Skeller & Henry Ford Sinclair came.
& we crossed our own red seas to get here,
fleeing a new Pharaoh with tobacco-stained teeth,
overseer of sweaty washwomen squeezing brown suds
into their tubs.

II

Why do they call it Dreamland? when every night
the same nightmare wakes you—your body hanging
from a tree limb, turning in the honey-moon.
You hear someone saying,

> *Did everyone get his keepsake?*
> *A button from his coat?*
> *A shoe?*
> *A tooth?*

Then you hear another voice call out,
Don't let any white man run it over you,

but fight!

You wake to hear Dick Rowland left
his shoeshine stand, tripped into Sarah Page
in an elevator, & started a riot.
He grabbed a white woman—or worse, they said.
To Lynch a Negro Tonight, the headline read.
Seventy-five strong left Greenwood with rifles,
pistols to make sure Dick Rowland kept his
buttons, his shoes, & his teeth.
*But fight! Don't let the white man
run it over you!*

III

Men drove into Greenwood with oil rags to set
fire to the world, pointed their rifles at firemen,
who could only hold their hoses & watch as Black
Wall Street burned.

For eighteen hours, our church house hymned
while smoke clouds rose & choked the skies
above Oklahoma.

For eighteen hours the Spirit rose in black smoke
& throttled our praise shouts.

Detroit, 1943

I

We came here to the Black Bottom,
Paradise Valley, on justice tickets for the Great
Migration, from the Bible Belt to the Black Belt—
from tobacco fields to the foundries of Ford,
to gaskets, rods, & burn-pocked faces laboring
over white-hot sparks. Lunchtime we ate our
soggy sandwiches & joked that we got hired
cause even the Devil himself up & quit, said
the work wasn't this hard in hell.

II

Dr. Sweet plucked weeds from his garden
& laughed with his wife: *If only weeds were prettier.*
We'd never have to plant a flower.
Better yet, she said, *we wouldn't have to pluck weeds.*

He watched his neighbors stare from the street,
their heads heavy like falling boulders.
They asked how he got to Garland Ave.
Years of setting bones & bussing tables, he answered.
He took an oath to do no man harm,
until he had to shoot one trying to pluck him
& Mrs. Sweet from their garden.

Nigger, you best go back to the Black Bottom,
or to the bottom of Black hell!

III

Who's safe when the police bring law & order
with a thousand rounds into a rooming house?
A man staggers to the curb cursing, his gut leaking.
But he was foolish in blood, & in love with the executioner.
He was determined to cross the redlines around the Motor
City & squint at the sunlight reflecting off bayonet tips.

Old Sparky

for George Stinney

State's youngest death
by electrocution: the executioner
in his olive-drab uniform moved
like an old middleweight.

In his breast pocket, a slip
of paper like a pocket square,
shopping list from home:
a pound of liverwurst, potatoes,
& green onions—a small bow
his wife drew beside the potatoes—
so this time he would not forget.

When the door opened,
there was the clank & groan
of steel; the condemned
shuffled in beside a guard with
bloodshot eyes & not a wrinkle
in his uniform.

The condemned, all ninety pounds,
stared at the rows of witnesses,
stared into the dark suits & dark ties,
boosted up by the Good Book
to the straps & metal skullcap, his tiny face,
shining as if honey-glazed, too small
for the death mask. & when the clock's
hands said 7:30, 2400 volts dimmed
the chamber bulb & jerked his mask away;

the 1900 that followed dimmed the chamber
bulb & jerked his 14 years away.

Monroe, NC, 1961

for Robert F. Williams

Picket signs & holes in marching shoe soles,
how I got over.
Face spit in at a lunch counter sit-in,
how I got over.
Ten days in jail, singing loud in my cell,
how I got over.
Hanged by the rope just to cast my one vote,
how I got over.
Protected my daughters & sons
with these here rifles & guns,
how I got over.

Philly, 1964

"A riot is the language of the unheard." – Martin Luther King Jr.

I

August made Columbia Ave. a brick oven.
When Fairmount Park exhaled, we found
our comfort in beer suds & Winstons
while windowsills blared horns from Motown:

All we need is music, sweet music,
& dancing in the street

Summer days were spent on stoops,
swatting hot air with church fans,
men leaning back in their chairs to eye
the hands they'd been dealt.

They made the exodus here to North Philly
from the tobacco crops of Carolina, Virginia,
& Mississippi. Some could still describe the sound
of rope tensing, & how a hog-bloated man bent
the limb of a red maple.

Reverend Cream had the first Cadillac
in the neighborhood & preached about a dream
where he saw Christ sitting with his disciples.
They had two bread loaves, two skins of wine, & three fish.
A firm believer in signs, he bet a dollar on
2-2-3 for a week straight. He had markings
on his face like Africans we saw on *National*
Geographic, but he liked to remind

the congregation, *Closest I ever been to Africa
is Harlem.*

II

We were the inheritors of those avenues,
Susquehanna, Columbia, & Lehigh,
by Connie Mack Stadium, where the crowds
swelled along 21st Street to watch the Phillies
chase a National League pennant.

Old Negro-leaguers like lefty
Sambo Sanders would come to
Connie Mack, rub his elbow & moan:

*Ballpark's the same as all over. Too many
Negroes movin' in 'round here. White folks
ain't at ease with things 'round the ballpark no more.*

Were you there in '47 when someone threw
a watermelon from the stands? They told
Jackie to enjoy it, but don't spit the seeds
on the field. Then the black cat they let loose
ran over the pitcher's mound & scampered
across home plate.

Let us stand for the National Anthem.
From his section, Sanders could hear
Chapman's Alabama drawl:

*Robinson, they may think you a
ballplayer, but you still a nigger to me!*

Jackie just knelt on one knee near the batter's box,
gazing into the outfield, elbow on his thigh,
choking the sweet spot of his bat.

III

Not a cloud in the sky over Will Penn,
five hundred & ten feet above rush hour.
For years he looked down on men from
Richard Allen to Strawberry Mansion pulled
from paddy wagons, their teeth knocked loose
with pistol butts. His bronze lips too heavy
to move as he looked down on 23rd & Columbia.

Lady, move that goddamned car!

& when the cops dragged Odessa
Bradford from her car, Will Penn watched.

You wouldn't drag a white woman like that!

Men came from every pew & watering hole
to tie fire to the Avenue, to Metzer's Pawnshop,
to Cohen's Furniture—& for three days,
North Philly burned like Sunday-sermon-hell.

A black cloud twisted over Columbia Ave.
& above Center Square, Will Penn watched.

New York, 1964

The Apollo marquee was like light from heaven.
After a taste or two, we'd go see Moms Mabley play,
or catch ol' Redd Foxx smoke-smothered on stage.
He kept the crowd rolling in their seats,
& when the theater doors opened,
laughter thundered uptown in Harlem.

Down on East 76th, Patrick Lynch used
a patched-up hose, leaking from a dozen holes
to spray the stoop & the Black boys sitting on it.

I'll wash you dirty niggers clean!

Was it only a schoolboy's laughter that sparked
New York? & where was the knife Lt. Gilligan
said he saw? The same knife in the hand of every
boy the police shot in New York. Boys whose stories
they scratched in notepads.

No one saw any knives, we told them.
But they kept asking anyway.

They didn't see any flames, they told us.
But we kept asking anyway.

Audubon Ballroom, 1965

"We are living in a time of revolution." – Malcolm X

I

He leaned into the microphone,
& the words came from the corner
of his mouth, feedback piercing my ears:
  As-salaam alaykum.
  Get your hand out my pocket!
A call & response, before the shotgun's
bald cry tore through the rostrum.

II

We washed his arms to the elbows,
rubbed his Detroit red goatee with musk,
shrouded the body in a white cocoon,
& four times raised our cupped hands:
  Allahu Akbar!
Then, with our shovels, we dug up dirt,
& with our palms, we filled the earth.

Newark, 1967

I

They carried two of every kind on the New Ark.
Pairs multiplied into the masses crowding
the corners of Springfield & Bergen, mecca
for Ralph Masters who stumbled into Post Drugstore
to find any relief from a molar tooth black as coal,
for Simeon Hobbs in Universal Shoes complaining
about wing tips a half-size too small.

Then the patriarchs made an exodus from the city,
hauling pieces of their enclaves to the edges of Essex
County, to make room for unwelcome neighbors.

The county fathers tore the map in pieces, leaving the city
nothing but scraps of paper on a table; the New Deal
redlining white flight to Short Hills & Millburn; landlords
leaving behind hanging gutters & lead piping.

II

Do you remember when the New Ark landed
on the Jersey shore in the shadow of Manhattan?
When they raised the project towers of Hayes Homes
brick by brick over Springfield & Bergen, crowded us
floor above floor like Babel? Left to wander past the rusting
fences of empty factories & their smokeless chimneys.
Then Stokely came & stood before the crowd at UCC:
In every other city, he said, *they're afraid of revolution!*
But in Newark, they don't even fear you!

They didn't heed him, even when murmurs turned to curses, even when pleas turned to threats. They thought we were just talking when we told them we might just have to tear this shit hole to the ground.

Making a Molotov cocktail

is simple. Almost any bottle will do,
Thunderbird, Manischewitz, but stay
clear of Coke bottles—thick glass don't
break so easy. Next you need some gas.
Siphon it from a parked car or take it from
a pump overnight. Careful filling 'em.
The fumes'll burn the hell out your eyes.

Cap the bottle; now all you need's a wick-fuse.
Tear up an old T-shirt, one with hard, yellow armpits.
Cut it in strips & wrap the bottles. Dunk 'em in
the gas till the strips are soaked—make sure
everything's tight. Then when *you* tight, it's ready.

Poison Olivetti

"Everywhere I look, Lord / I see FB eyes."

— Richard Wright, "The FB Eye Blues"

At my desk, planted
deep in files & boxes
of revolutionaries,
I turn the knob on my Olivetti
& type a letter to a wife:
Dear Clara...
  Dear Coretta...
a letter to a former ally:
Malcolm...
  Elijah...

a newspaper headline:
Number Two in Organization Eyes
Number One Spot

a letter to a Nobel Prize winner

King, In view of your low grade...

At my desk, planted deep
in typewriter ribbon, fingers
blue with venomous ink,
I drink Red Label, transcribe secret
hotel room tapes, & fill envelopes
with the anonymity of a life's work.

Lorraine Motel, 1968

The echo of this rifle shot
like a voice from the burning
bush. Said the voice:
Remove thy shoes & pray.

Heavy the head that wears the crown—
Lord, may this bullet lighten his burden.

Washington, DC, 1968

Tanny Miller did the work
of the Hellfighters, carried rifle
& bolo across French fields,
came home & paraded the avenues
uptown in Harlem, Croix de Guerre
& the rattlesnake on his chest—steel
plate in his foot.

He looked out on the National Guard
doing the work of LBJ, carrying machine
guns & gas masks down U Street. Something
so familiar in their eyes, the look of the Krauts.

War saps the syrupy sweet from men, he thought,
& now DC would ooze dark & sticky like molasses.

Chicago, 1969

for Fred Hampton

I do not love mine
enemy or his 4 a.m.
raids, his blasting up
my hall, his bullets
through my wall, his
holes through my bed,
his two holes in my head.

I do not love mine enemy
or the pigs who come to
kill you in your sleep
& do not give you time
to turn your cheek.

Attica, 1971

I

They packed this prison like a slave ship, the gun
tower sailing the skies above Attica like a crow's nest.
Granite ships: sliding gates & cement walls raised high
over the fields & trees. The guards jingle corridor keys
that turn the locks to a man's guts—men, bald &
gray as cement, & harder. Prison is the cycle of life:

> *someone enters, someone dies—*
> *another dies, another enters.*

The hole is the hold of this ship; you hear the waters
rush beneath you & plan an escape from your skull.
Has anyone ever made it over the wall? Or tunneled
the labyrinth under their skin to the heart caged
somewhere between their ribs, a hole deeper than this,
this box beneath Attica?

II

The guards will swear on whatever book
you put in front of them that no one screams
in the hole, that only animals go to the hole
(& even animals don't howl in the hole, they say).
So every screw gets a chair & a whip, a heel & a baton.

They are big game hunters in the gun towers,
waiting for word from beyond the walls
of this preserve, from the halls of Rockefeller:
It's all a Black thing, Mr. President.

Time to separate the sheep from the goats.

III

In D-yard, they speak the literal
language of the cell, their fists, their fros
knotted wall to wall. But up in the gun towers,
they speak the ironies of the warden:
Give up, & you won't be harmed!

Watts Writers Workshop, 1973

A Watts Love Story, read the subtitle.
They found it that night, a half-burned
page, some lines, some dialogue,
some notes scribbled in the margins.
It begins with a character named Shake
& his wife Lena sitting in their kitchen:

> *(They sit at a white Formica table.
> LENA pours coffee from a small
> coffee pot)*

> SHAKE: I don't care what your
> Mama said. I ain't thinkin' about
> runnin' off with that woman.

> LENA: *(Scoffs & rises from her
> chair)* Runnin' off one thing. Shackin'
> up is somethin' entirely different. Now
> ain't it?

There, the page browns—then blackens,
& the couple's story ends.

All night, poets & playwrights scoured the burnt remains:
chairs & desks & sofa cushions, but not another word
about Shake & Lena to be found. Theirs is a tragedy
forever in flames.

LA, 1992

"To get some respect, we had to tear this motherfucker up."

— Ice Cube

I

Whatchu buy?

What you watch us buy here every day:
soap, coffee, cigarettes, the dollar-seventy-nine
bottle of orange juice you shot Latasha over.

We drive slow down Normandie,
by another man's face on
the asphalt, prostrate like some saint.
Black boot on his neck, shotgun
to his cheek, lips moving like a supplicant.

Why is he facedown
                              on the City of Angels?
Who is he praying to?

But the police are here to do their
duty: to serve, protect, & strip
him to his bare ass on the sidewalk—
there is law & order in his nakedness.
The helicopters above him
cut the sky to pieces. But shelter
from what falls today will be expensive.
It will cost them their dead presidents
& 8,000 boots on the ground. Today,

31

they pay full price for our nakedness.

II

The two words echoed through the streets,
through Watts & Compton, louder than
bloodhounds in the woods of Georgia, louder
than hoses washing marchers down the streets
of Selma, Birmingham, & Oxford, louder than
the rifle fire from a gun tower above Attica,
louder than dynamite blasting through 16th Street
Baptist, through four little girls, loud as Rodney
King's silent video capturing a thousand nights
on a thousand dark streets.

We heard the words over the alarms,
the sirens, the choppers:

Not Guilty
         Not Guilty
Not Guilty

Words that fractured the fault line running
through Simi Valley, but when the ground
began to quake, they felt nothing. It was down
in South Central that the earth threw up its burden
beneath our feet. We bounced & swayed through
the rumbles with everything we could carry:
a blender, a microwave, a stereo.
From the pulpits & lecture halls, they asked,
What is wrong down there?
Why does the ground shake like that?
But in the streets, we were catching our footing

& watching a hundred buildings turn to ash.

Can't we all get along?

& we answered with a block of concrete,
an exhaust pipe, a shotgun, with gas & rags.
We answered with Reginald Denny,
with Fidel Lopez.

The ground shook us loose, like a man from his chains,
& we too kept shaking, until it all fell down,
until the earth threw us up, along with its burden.

The Real Cold Killers: A Novel

for Amadou Diallo

I used to think
Chester Himes
was the greatest of
all crime novelists,

until I read
the fiction
of Sean Carrol,
Kenneth Boss,
Richard Murphy, &
Edward McMellon.

II

"You all know how Black humor started? It started in slave ships. Cat was over there rowing. Dude say, 'What you laughin' about?' Said, 'Yesterday I was a king.'"

— Richard Pryor

Barnstormers

"They used to say, 'If we find a good Black player, we'll sign him.'
They was lying." – Cool Papa Bell

They tell me Pop was some ballplayer.
Copper-toned, tan as the leather of his glove,
squinting on a dirt mound under Virginia skies.

A southpaw they tell us.
Tall & slight—the way a pitcher should be.
His lanky arms made his wind & release like a slingshot.

Fingers curled in a question mark for knucklers.
A little tobacco spit made his sinkers spiral & drop
over the plate like a yo-yo. They say his mud ball
would have put the Babe on his ass.

At Mama's, I sometimes stare at his creased
photo fading in the family album & think to myself,
He sure don't look like much: tattered logo & numbers
coming apart at the seams.

They were Pullman-porters who clanked dishware
on sleeping cars, barnstorming every city from Tupelo
to Hackensack & warming up in bullpens beside chicken fence.

Cheers from the crowds became the cries
of eleven children & ship horns on the docks
of the Navy Yard. We played peek-a-boo
at his funeral beneath the pews of 19th Street Baptist,
too little to care anything about the cancer
he coughed up for months.

They say he always joked that when he died,
he was gon' haunt them ballparks the way they did
in the days when he & his tribe were just
shadows of the game.

Osage Ave.

My best Superfly Snuka
off the dining room table,
put my little cousin Jerm in a half nelson,
then a pile driver from the banister.
We knocked over chairs & slammed
into Mom Midgy's china closet.
When her crystal & plates clinked, she stumbled
from the kitchen with an extension cord,
threatening to give our legs a shock if we
didn't get from her house. We slammed
into each other like a game of roughhouse
in the tiny vestibule trying to be the first one out.

We spilled off the porch into the heated
May evening & sprinted up Tasker Street
around the corner to Two Guy's
to buy Tastykakes, Boston Baked Beans,
& Lemonheads. Whenever the door jingled,
Mackey never took an eye off us; he always
mumbled through cigarette smoke that
South Philly boys were born crooked.
I bought a pickle from the murky jar on the counter
& listened to the old heads huddled around
the 14" Emerson on milk crates. They guzzled
Old English in twisted paper bags & slurred
at the scene on the TV— a furnace-black cloud swelling
over West Philly, fire trucks parked along the block,
                    hoses coiled.
They done dropped a bomb on them niggers.
I tore the top off my Lemonheads & shook
some in my mouth. Leaving the store, we headed

to the stoop to pitch quarters,
arguing over who would win a rumble
between the Hulk & the Thing.

Ask the Local Gentrification

How many bricks did they turn to dust last year
when they imploded our building? When the city
lined the streets with dumpsters, came in with cranes,
wrecking balls, & C4?

Through the brown cloud, I remembered
all those mailboxes missing names & numbers.
Our mailman was some kind of savant.

Ms. Pat, who wore a different wig every day
& at night kept her teeth in a pickle jar beside her bed.
Mr. Ralph, who gave us rolls of quarters to bring him packs
of Kool's from Two Guys. He used to chase us down
the halls, until MS tangled up his legs.

Ms. Tink, who grew a garden on her 5th floor balcony.
Her reds, pinks, & greens were like Eden above our asphalt
earth. August days, Uncle Peo brought out the plug wrench
& turned the corner into Wild Water Kingdom.

We splashed until the water department trucks came to dry us
out, stood there dripping & grinning, knowing those trucks
would have to come right back.

This was all before the brown cloud,
before the coffee shops & dog groomers came,
before the bulldozers, moving vans, & U-Hauls
carted our lives away, one lampshade
& china closet at a time.

5th Floor Cooper

I only wanted to get to the 5th floor,
but when I got on the elevator
I saw the way she clutched her bag,

as if it were her first born,
flesh of her flesh. Truth told,
the bag *was* exquisite.

Black crocodile
with a diamond latch—
I'm sure it was a Birkin.

I know because my wife wants one,
& as much as I know she'd love to have it,
I needed to get to the 5th floor.

When the doors slid shut,
she flashed that filtered
Instagram smile,

voice cracked like a bad signal
when she said hello, one eye on me
the other on emergency.

As each floor lit up, she inched
farther & farther into the corner of the car.
Maybe, I should have just given her

what she expected, big-footed Mandingo
with his fist around her throat
right there on the elevator floor.

At least then she could have justified her fears.
But then I would have been late,
& I really needed to get to the 5th floor.

Dogmen

I

From an unfinished basement,
hoarse barks rise to prove
they're game, turning in circles,
& running along the cages; 14,000
years has readied them for the pit.

My Jezebel is a game bitch—
tiger-striped red-nose Colby,
forty-three pounds of lean muscle,
head like a ham, sired by Mojo from
the line of the great Mudbone,
but neither of them half
the scrapper she is.

For the keep, she runs the treadmill,
lolls her tongue & laps the froth
that drips & sticks to her coat,
or pulls a shopping cart full of
cinderblocks like a mule cart.

For quickness we toss stray tabbies
in the yard & feed her raw meatballs
seasoned with gunpowder,

    raw meat
for the taste of blood,
    gunpowder
for fire in the belly.

II

Fight night, I pack saline solution
for scars, needle & thread for stitches,
a surgeon in my stained T-shirt closing
gashes above her ear. But even cut up
in a scrape, she wags for me. I rub her
chest so she can feel my care.

I pull her from the cage, face turned
from her opponent; runners shout bets
& collect wrinkled bills. I unmuzzle her
& whisper, *That's my bitch. You get 'er, girl.*

When the ref slaps the mat & yells *Let 'em go!*
I unloose hell. They rise on hind legs,
all gums & incisors, all eyes as her jaws
take hold; she catches the other dog's
throat & shakes until it sags—either dying,
or spirit broken.

We pry Jezebel loose & wipe
the cuts on her face. For her,
it is not about spoils or boasts.
She does it out of instinct, &
for the survival of all canid.

Castled

The ex-con sat at the park tables & told us how
he'd seen a man die in a prison mess hall.
Cook beat him to death with a soup pot, he said.
Something to do with a bug in his stew. Cook told
the boy to just eat it, it was full of protein.
The old man could tell a story, as colorful as the leaves
circling the park. But he forgets. The last time he
told it, the cook hadn't killed him, he had only
broken his jaw with a ladle.

But we believed every word he said about the lifer
the guards dragged out the hole after one year, who
said the demons who lived behind his toilet bowl
had pissed all over the walls. The infirmary had to
force-feed him his meds. Red Thorazine, he swore,
were the Devil's baby teeth.

The old man sacrificed his bishop & told us how he never
lost a game in the joint, except to a guy who got himself
raped in the laundry. *What kind of person beats somebody
who'd already lost so much?* he asked & let him win in six
moves, but it didn't stop him from twisting his neck up
in his bedsheets.

Ruined a perfect record for nothing, he said.
Kid could've beat Bobby Fischer & still would've hung hisself.

I shuddered at the wind & tapped over my king.
As the old man went to resetting the pieces, he
rolled up his sleeve to show us the tattoo he got
a week before coming home:

*The Lotus Flower Grows
from the Deepest Mud*

The Plans

Hunched over the plans, thumb
& index pinching the bridge of his nose,
mumbling all to be damned.

Me, over his shoulders, flag in my hand rocking
back & forth, looking at the shapes & dotted
lines that meant me racing a blue Huffy down Tasker Street.

Floor full of pliers, vice grips, a butter knife, & a hammer—
    a hammer in case all else failed.

A kitchen of handlebars, rubber grips, spokes,
Chains, & a fifth of Southern Comfort. In his hand,
instructions smudged with chain grease.

A sad chain just sagged from the gears,
& no matter how long he spun the pedals
or how many swigs he took from the bottle,
it remained a U.

I remember it now, hunched over my daughter's
dollhouse, cracking plastic ties, grunting
like a small ape.

She, on the tip of her toes behind me,
the diagrams & charts that mean
her putting Barbie to bed.

A floor full of tiny shutters, doors, bathtubs,
balusters, spiral staircases, lattice,
bags of screws, & silver duct tape—

duct tape, in case all else fails.

A spiteful roof that keeps collapsing,
& no matter how many threads I strip,
it remains a V.

Looney Tunes

My father was a blue-jawed drunk.
A pint of Southern Comfort, & he'd
wipe his mouth with the back of his hand.
You could smell Bluto seeping from his pores.

He'd take a hammer, two-by-four, even a shotgun
& run you out of the house & into a yard full of snow,
rootin' tootin' like Yosemite Sam.

I wondered would the neighbors have chuckled
if he'd blown our faces to ash, nothing left but our
eyes blinking behind gun smoke.

My mother's skull sounded like a gong
when he smacked her with a skillet,
like when Jerry would crack Tom across the head.
I stared at the knot that rose from her forehead,
looking for the stars & little birdies to circle it.

Is It Something He Said?

When I snuck past my father, he was all over the couch
mumbling a drunk man's dream & crunching
the plastic cover with every turn. But no matter how
much he crunched, not a drop spilled from the pint
of Southern Comfort on his chest.

I fumbled with the diamond knob on the basement
door & creaked down the stairs into the red-light district.
When I stubbed my toe on the washing machine, it
rumbled through the house like a dump truck—but not
a peep from Pops. So, I flipped through the stacks of albums
in milk crates—& there, tucked between Donny Hathaway
& the Ohio Players, the bushy afro & wild man's smile:

> *Ladies & Gentlemen, the one & only Richard Pryor!*
& as the record spun, I heard my neighborhood in every
groove.

> *Bartender, nigga give me my whiskey!*
& I could see Uncle Bill coming out of Basin's Lounge,
stumble across Tasker Street & slump over the hood of his car,
mistaking his pant leg for a toilet bowl.

> *Officer, I -am -reaching -into -my -pocket —for-my -license!*
& I could see Pops moving *real* slow for his wallet the night
some state troopers pulled us over in Jersey.

> *You don't know how to deal with the Whiteman. That's your
> problem.*
& I could see Scoop drinking Malt Duck on 24th Street,
going on about trickle-down economics, giving the kind

of wisdom only a wino can.

      Did ya'll see The Exorcist? It's a story about the Devil...
& there I was in the Roxy with my sister,
our feet in the seats. While the mice scuttled
beneath us, we watched this crazy girl throw up pea
soup & twist her head around.

The whole time, I kept one ear on Pops upstairs
& one on Pryor, sounding like our fathers, our uncles,
our neighbors—our junkies, & sat there wondering
why they hid him from us in basements.

The Lincoln of Letters

"The nigger, like the Injun, will be eliminated: it is the law of races, history, what-not." – Walt Whitman

I have squirmed in my seat since my 2nd grade teacher Ms. Cherry threw a reading workbook at my bowed head, nested in the warmth & darkness of the valley between my forearms & shoulders.
In those days, teachers treated us like prison labor.

In high school, we were sentenced to four years of Poe, Pound, Eliot, & Dickinson, while the only poets I wanted to study were Rakim, Big Daddy Kane, & Kool G Rap.

In grad school, I broke the rocks of the Romantics but knew Brooks & Dumas were waiting for me at the gates.
Africa has left us no classic poets, a classmate said.
The canon is of Europe & the New World.
& by *us* he meant Milton, Yeats—& himself.

Another student leaned over to me like we were in a confessional & whispered so low I almost had to read his lips. *Where he get that bullshit from?* I tapped the cover of our anthology like a hand drum & scoffed.
Maybe Whitman.

Graveyard of Poets

I slid the papers across their desks,
& the mood in the room grew somber
as a wake. They hated poetry, & the hypocrite
in me hated to have to teach it to them.

Corey lifted the paper in front of him,
a white veil beneath his eyes.
Who Walt Whitman? he asked.
A poet from Camden, I replied.
He unveiled his face, tight as a charley horse:
Don't no poets live here.

He didn't know that Whitman has been
entombed a hundred & twenty years in two
granite stones fixed in a hillside, the initials of
pilgrim poets carved in the trees all around him.

I mention Whitman's tomb is in Harleigh, & Corey
looked up from the poem: *My brother buried there.*
& I remembered his brother, how he used to cut
up in my class, tapping on his desk & rhyming under
his breath half the period.

Then I imagined his brother's grave, a headstone
no bigger than a cinder block—no trees, no initials.
How many pilgrim poets have passed his grave
& never read his name or stopped to carve theirs?

& how many times has Corey passed the stones
of the gray poet, leaves of fresh cut grass staining
the soles of his shelltops?

Love in the Time of Corona

Nights like tonight, I live off two-day-old
rice delivered from Hayun's. Nina in the back
room calling me sinner man. I squat at the foot
of the bed near piles of laundry,

shirts & pants stuffed in pillowcases,
& take sips from a bottle making another ring
on the nightstand. I barely notice the stacks
of yellowed newspapers in the kitchen
or the paperbacks' curled up pages by the vestibule door.

I keep your key in the penny jar at the top
of the closet, next to the empty shoe boxes.
Where are all those shoes?
Too many hangers for such a tiny closet.
Tomorrow I'll try to get up & throw some out.

But tonight, the wind coming through
the cardboard taped to the window
reminds me it's April, & the weight of my
breath reminds me of the wind in March.

A Lightweight Irony

Cut man
puts a Q-tip
behind his ear,
grabs an
end-swell
& a gob of
Vaseline
with two fingers,
& slides it across
the lightweight's
blow-fished face.
In sixty seconds,
he closes a gash,
shrinks a mouse,
& wipes a stream
of blood from
the fighter's cheek,
only to send
him back out
there for more
of the same.

Word Problems

When do you know you're a poet & not a mathematician?
When you sit in Mr. Masker's class & he reads,
*Timmy has $10.38 in his pocket. He buys two cans of sardines for 53¢
each, a bag of salt & vinegar potato chips for $1.24, & a dill pickle
for 96¢. How many nickels does Timmy get back in change?*

But you have no interest in the numbers, only the narrative.
You picture Timmy, short, hands too small for his body.
He loves Three Stooges reruns & secretly listens to KISS.

He fakes a Brooklyn accent to rebel against suburbia
& has been in love with a girl named Sparky since she moved
up the block. You know his backstory, his conflict, what's
at stake—but for the life of you, you can't figure out how
many nickels the cashier just dropped in his palm.

Sugar Shack

I found Marvin's "I Want You"
in my father's box marked *Midnight Magic.*
I followed the beam of white light
drowning the dusky figures
twisting in every direction:
women with their skirts pulled up,
thighs like drumsticks, heels nailed
to the wooden planks; men with their wiry
arms stretched to the cross beams,
eyes shut to the ecstasy around them.
Only one man in a wrinkled blue uniform
sits hunched over on a chair, a bottle at his feet,
too drunk to join the jubilee. Above him on stage,
the conked lead singer has the whole shack in rapture.

Judgment Day

Rush hour traffic inches past him.
He holds half a Starbuck's coffee
cup & a reminder scrawled in bold
red on a piece of cardboard:
    ARE YOU READY?

He put his face in the cracked
window of a white Land Rover.
The driver leaned almost into
the passenger seat, eyes wide as
a silent film star. She closed
the window & waved him off.

The hole in his shoe showed
the hole in his sock; the hole in his
sock showed the missing toes.
Veteran of some long-forgotten
conflict, he once taught kids
integers & equations at Woodrow
Wilson High, now a seer at a highway
off-ramp, plucking out the little white
serpents he says sliver in his beard.

He passed slowly in front of her car
as the light turned green. She mouthed
something intense & dramatic à la Lilian Gish
& gave it gas. He sat on the curb & pressed
his marker on the back of the cardboard sign:
    THOUGH IT TARRIES, WAIT FOR IT...

The Explorer

Van Hook, 2 a.m.

Volvo wagon
docks in unchartered darkness.
Cherry Hill math teacher lands
in Centerville to discover
the land of coke & Hippolyta.

Head on a swivel, knuckles white
as pearls from his grip on the wheel.
He's wide-eyed paranoia behind
the windshield, but not enough
to keep him moored in suburbia.

Maybe
it's the thrill of the unknown around
those corners, the two minutes of
non-missionary in the back seat.

Maybe
it's the explorer's spirit,
the Columbus & Vespucci in him—
the love of exotic spices,
dark jungles, & restless natives.

Ray's Original Styling

Crossing Mickle Boulevard,
I can hardly read the sign,
faded red & white bubble
letters: RAY's.

The steps squeak like rocking
chairs, & the stairwell smells
like burnt wood, smoke
curling from a stick of incense
like a séance.

Saturday mornings, the shop
is always loud as gang war,
& there are hairs everywhere—
on the wobbly chairs, the
checkered floor, our white T's,
& the tips of our tongues.

The barber's smock is stained
with clipper oil & hair grease.
He shuffles the hard plastic combs,
boar-bristled brushes, razors,
& blow-dryers around his station.
Cords wind & wiggle
like jungle vines.

A father wrestles his son
into the barber's chair.
The clippers sound like
a hive in his ear, & sometimes
they sting like a hive.

Ray shapes & sculpts—
doing everything he can to keep
his clay still. He looks up into his
mirrors, smudged with fingerprints.

What could he possibly see?
What is there to see anyway?

Nothing but fingerprints & hair,
     curly, kinky,
matted, puffy
hair, & a hamper of damp, dingy
white towels beside the wash bowl.

In the corner, there is an ancient
Dubble Bubble machine with a few
gumballs hard as marbles, & a peeling
yellow sticker: *Gum 25¢*.

The Exorcist's Song

It's true.
I witnessed an exorcism once.
It was everything you'd imagine:
the smells, the vomit, cursing Christ in tongues—
but with all of that, I couldn't take my eyes
off the possessed man's mismatched socks.

Were they, too, from the whispers of Satan?
The priest didn't seem to notice.
He was busy with scripture,
holy water, & waving his cross.

Different colors might have been bearable,
but one tube & one dress was ungodly.
It took three of us to hold him down on the bed.

& I was horrified at his blaspheming all that is holy,
but how I wanted— (Son of man, how I wanted!)
to loose those socks from his feet
more than the demons from his soul.

Doll Baby

India,
all eyes through the aisles
of toys:
Crazy Balls & Silly Putty
in front of the glossy boxes of Barbie:
Not that one, Daddy, the pretty one,
golden locks & crystal eyes
like Cinderella,
Snow White

India
wishes she
was a pretty doll, too,
honey hair & crystal eyes
like Cinderella,
snow white

Yakub's Creation

Legend has it that 6,600
years ago, on the Island
of Patmos, Yakub began
grafting the colored man
from the Asiatic Black.

6,600 years later,
on the Island of Manhattan,
Black Barbie selfies
in a platinum wig
& blue contacts—
still dissatisfied,

still killing
the darker
germ.

Sacagawea

His guitar sounded like a ukulele.
But the way he strummed it, you
would swear it belonged to B.B.
before he ran off with Lucille.

The corner of 4th & South his stage,
& me, his audience— I tossed what
change I had on the red felt of his
guitar case. *God bless,* he said in key.
He looked down at the offering,
& after a chord or two, he sang:

> *When they gon' put Ida B. on some money?*
> *When they gon' put Harriet on that twenty?*

Whitman Park

is a field of
tin fossils,
not a statue

in miles,
not a dot
on a state

map.
Asphalt broken
up

under years
of falling sky,
yet brilliant

with broken
glass, like pieces
of diamond

& emerald,
mined
from Carool's

liquor store.
Pigeons cluster &
warble near the stumps

of trees we once climbed,
where dogs barked at each
other & turned in circles

over chicken bones.
No other eyes but mine
to fall on what's left

of Whitman Park—
its precious gems &
chicken bones.

Black Velveteen

There were no runways along
her Southside asphalt.
Only the squared numbers
for hopscotch informed

the walk that lights
the New York stage,
Hottentot Venus
of fashion week.

Black Velveteen under
the display of the lens
& white lights of
the millennium.
She is dusky as God's tribe.

Black Velveteen,
flanked by the angelic
boy-hipped daughters
of the New World,

turns on a stiletto
like she did in a schoolyard,
one leg high, holding a broken
piece of chalk in her hand.

Portraits

When he was sober, he was
something of an artist. With pencils
& charcoal, he brought the eyes
of Ali & King to life above
the fireplace mantel: eyes that followed
you across the room & made you
move fast through the kitchen
doorway on a late-night cereal run.

It also made you afraid of the thumbs
that put life into those stares —rubbing
& smudging the pages.

I hadn't been in his house in twenty years.
Hadn't wanted to see him or those eyes,
but still I came & sat at the table to hear
talk of divvying up the attic & basement:
antique clocks & china wear.

He lies somewhere in Banks Funeral
Home, eyes emptier than his creations.
& I hoped he didn't leave me any of it,
not the attic or the basement or the thumb-
smudged pages—& certainly not those eyes.
They had spooked me far too long.

Burner

for Dondi

If crumbling concrete was your
only canvas, you'd wait for nightfall
to lug Krylon in a canvas duffle bag just
to hear the sound of creation: the hiss
& rattle of can strokes in the yard.

You'd start with a slanted outline
in midnight black—ten feet high,
then fill it in with blues & grays &
whites: a sky shattering like glass.
You'd add a blood orange sun exploding
into skyscrapers above wildstyle letters:
   Arsons at Large
& beside it, a goldenrod scroll unfolding:
   Still...
   In 2 It

Two Moons

Mansa woke chained in the hold of the *Gallito*.
Arms & legs shackled with Spanish steel.
He could only press his ear to the wood planks to hear
the sea rush, black & endless, below the schooner,
troubled as the night above the masts, troubled
as the darkness in the hold.

Before the trouble, Mansa sat cross-legged in the fields.
While he tracked the sun's descent, smoke spiraled
from clay cook pots, & the tall grass prostrated to the winds.

He climbed the mountain passageways till his spear
almost parted the clouds, descending only as
the moon mirrored in the streams.

Then at the foot of the hills, he was captured
in rope & net, bound & tied by men
of the western tribes, then driven across
the countryside, driven till his feet split,
even then driven.

& when the morning sky faded a thousand stars,
he saw the wall along the coast.
Through the barracoon bars, he watched
fleets rocking in their moorings, awaiting
the inspection of goods: rumps & rum,
molars & molasses, shoulders & silver.

He heard the chant of the traders
until two moons waned.
The chant he heard above all prayer—
América! América!

Chronological Notes

1906: After newspapers printed unsubstantiated reports that four white women were raped, allegedly by African American men, white mobs gathered in downtown Atlanta & went throughout the business district assaulting Black people. White vigilante groups then went into Black neighborhoods to attack their residents. At least twenty-five African Americans & two whites died in the riots.

1919: On July 27, in Chicago, Illinois, seventeen-year-old Eugene Williams was swimming in Lake Michigan with friends. After crossing the unofficial barrier between the white side & Black side, whites began to throw stones at Williams. Struck in the head by a stone, he drowned & died. When police refused to arrest the man responsible for killing Williams, an angry mob gathered on the beach. An altercation occurred in which a white police officer was shot. This set off several days of violence. In the end, fifteen whites & twenty-three Blacks died.

1921: For approximately eighteen hours (May 31 – June 1), white mobs attacked Black residents in the Greenwood section of Tulsa, Oklahoma. During the attack, they burned down the thriving business district known as Black Wall Street Officially, twenty-six Blacks & ten whites were killed in the violence.

1943: After rumors spread that a white woman had been raped, a mob of whites attacked several Black men as they left the Roxy Theater in Detroit, Michigan. Violent attacks erupted throughout the city, but it was only after white gangs entered the Black section of Paradise Valley that 6,000 army troops in tanks were sent in to quell the violence. Twenty-five Blacks & nine whites died in the riots.

1944: On June 16, fourteen-year-old George Stinney became the youngest American to be executed. At 7:30 p.m., he was put to death by electric chair. Seventy years later, in 2004, his conviction was overturned.

1961: In August, the Freedom Riders came to Monroe, North Carolina, to protest local segregation laws. During the protests, white citizens grew hostile with the Riders. Robert F. Williams & his Black Guard were called & came to aid the Riders.

1964: After holding up traffic at the intersection of 23rd Street & Columbia Avenue. in North Philadelphia, police tried to physically remove Odessa Bradford from her car. Witnessing the incident, a bystander attempted to come to her defense, but both were arrested. Rumors spread that a pregnant Black woman had been beaten to death by police, & as a result, residents looted & burned white-owned businesses in the neighborhood. Although no one was killed, at least three hundred & forty people were injured.

1964: Riots erupted in Harlem, New York, after fifteen-year-old James Powell was shot & killed by a white off-duty police officer. This resulted in a six-day uprising that spread from Harlem to the Bedford Stuyvesant section of Brooklyn. One person died, & over one hundred others were injured.

1965: On February 21, Malcolm X was assassinated in the Audubon Ballroom in Harlem, New York.

1967: After John William Smith, a Black taxicab driver in Newark, New Jersey, was brutally beaten & arrested by two white officers, he was taken to the 4th Police Precinct & charged with assaulting the officers. Back in Haynes Homes, rumors spread that Smith had been beaten to death while in police custody. A large crowd gathered outside the precinct, & an altercation between police & the crowd occurred. Then, on July 12, during a rally protesting Smith's beating, unrest broke out. After six days of rioting, at least twenty-five people were dead.

1968: On April 4, Martin Luther King Jr. was assassinated at the Lorraine Motel in Memphis, Tennessee.

1968: Following the assassination of Martin Luther King Jr., riots broke out in Washington, DC, at the corner of 14th & U streets. At least thirteen people were killed during the unrest.

1969: On December 4, Fred Hampton, Chairman of the Illinois chapter of the Black Panther Party for Self Defense, was assassinated by law enforcement officers during an early-morning raid of his home in Chicago, Illinois.

1971: After years of demanding better living conditions (& receiving news of the killing of George Jackson in San Quentin State Prison in California), over a thousand inmates at Attica State Prison revolted & gained control of the facility, taking approximately forty of the prison staff as hostages. During four days of negotiations, the authorities agreed to all the prisoners' demands except amnesty from prosecution. Governor Nelson Rockefeller then ordered the state police to storm the prison & put down the uprising. In the end, close to forty-three people were dead, including ten prison employees & thirty-three inmates.

1971: On March 8, a group known as the Citizens' Commission broke into the FBI offices in Media, Pennsylvania, & stole over one thousand classified documents—including poison pen letters, manuals, routine forms, etc.—exposing the Bureau's secret counterintelligence program COINTELPRO.

1973: During the summer months, a government informant named Darthard Perry (aka Othello) burned down the Watts Writers Workshop in Los Angeles, California, at the behest of his FBI handlers.

1992: After the beating of motorist Rodney King was caught on camera & broadcast around the world, images of King being tased, kicked, & struck with batons by a group of police officers enraged many in the community. Due to the public outcry, the LA District Attorney charged four officers with assault & excessive use of force. However, all four of the officers were acquitted. Uprisings erupted in Los Angeles, California. In the aftermath, sixty-three people were dead.

1999: On February 4, four plainclothes police officers fired a combined total of forty-one shots at an unarmed Amadou Diallo in the Bronx, New York, killing him. All four officers were later acquitted of second-degree murder & reckless endangerment.

ACKNOWLEDGMENTS

These poems have appeared, sometimes in different versions, in the following publications, whose editors I gratefully acknowledge:

Platform Review: "Word Problems," "Graveyard of Poets," "The Lincoln of Letters," & "Is It Something He Said?"
Exit 7: "Ask the Local Gentrification" & "Black Velveteen"
Four Way Review: "Barnstormers"
Southern Indiana Review: "Osage Ave."
Slush: "Two Moons"

I must also express gratitude to the mentors, teachers, family, & friends who helped make this volume possible with their patience, support, insight, &, most of all, their love.

I especially want to thank Pat Rosal, who has been my greatest advisor, editor, & confidante. I am ever grateful for the many days he spent reading these poems & giving me invaluable advice. His encouragement helped me get here.

About the Author

Malik Abduh is a poet & essayist. He earned an MFA in Creative Writing from Rutgers University-Camden, where he received the 2008 Rutgers University Alumni Association Writing Award. His work appears in several journals & magazines, including *Southern Indiana Review*, *Four Way Review*, *Exit 7*, *Slush*, & *Some Call it Ballin' Magazine*. He teaches English at Rowan College at Burlington County & is the editor of the College's journal, *The Baron Anthology*.